CHEER UP, SYDNEY

A Book about Compassion

Paula Bussard
Illustrated by Terry Julien

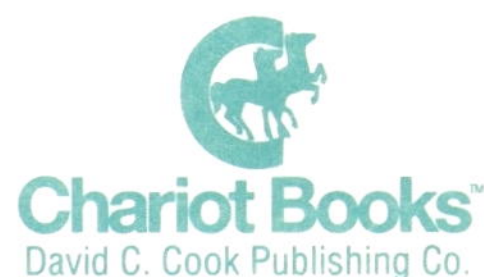

Chariot Books™
David C. Cook Publishing Co.

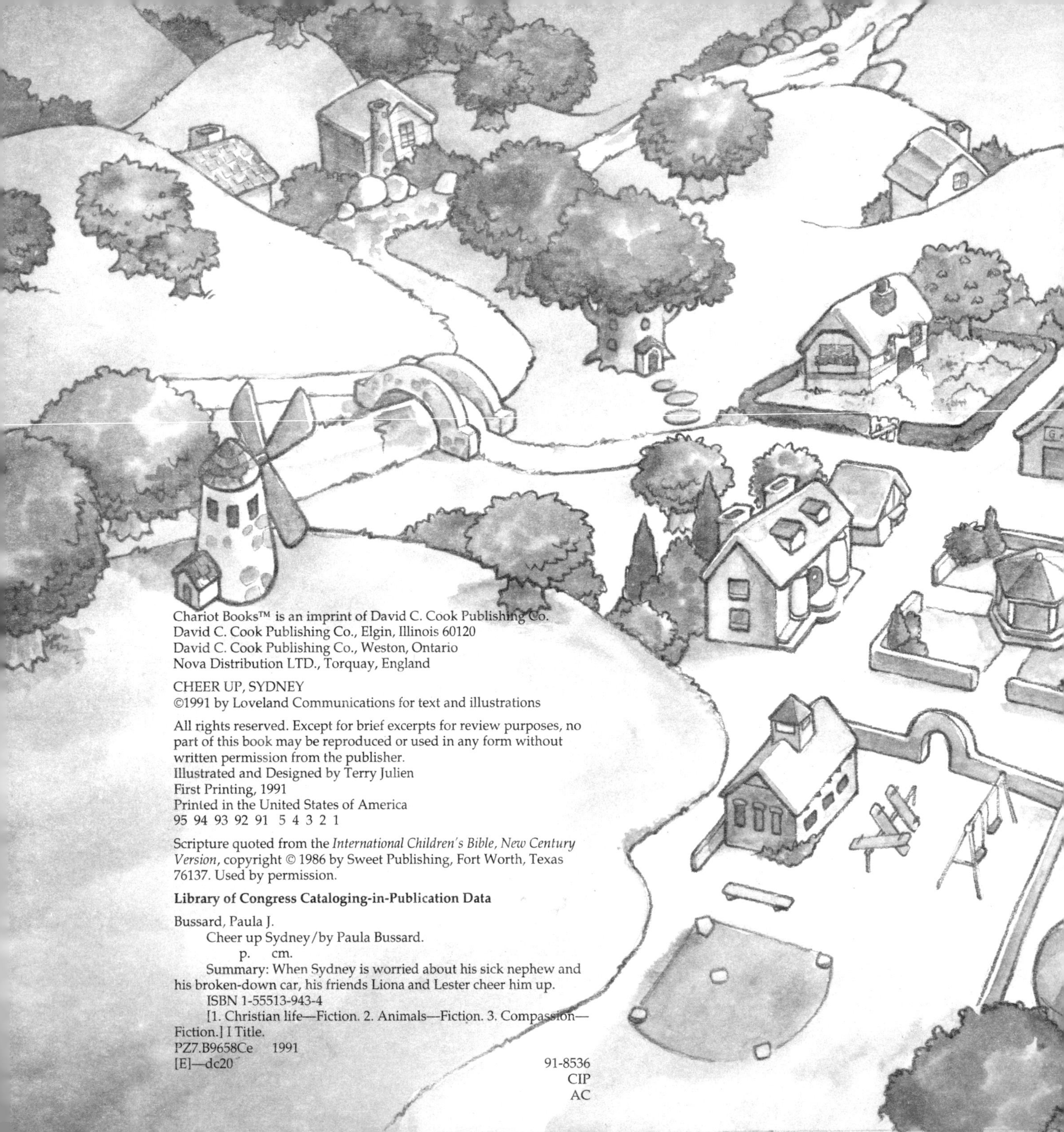

Chariot Books™ is an imprint of David C. Cook Publishing Co.
David C. Cook Publishing Co., Elgin, Illinois 60120
David C. Cook Publishing Co., Weston, Ontario
Nova Distribution LTD., Torquay, England

CHEER UP, SYDNEY
©1991 by Loveland Communications for text and illustrations

Illustrated and Designed by Terry Julien
First Printing, 1991
Printed in the United States of America
95 94 93 92 91 5 4 3 2 1

Scripture quoted from the *International Children's Bible, New Century
Version*, copyright © 1986 by Sweet Publishing, Fort Worth, Texas
76137. Used by permission.

Library of Congress Cataloging-in-Publication Data

Bussard, Paula J.
    Cheer up Sydney/by Paula Bussard.
        p.   cm.
    Summary: When Sydney is worried about his sick nephew and
his broken-down car, his friends Liona and Lester cheer him up.
    ISBN 1-55513-943-4
    [1. Christian life—Fiction. 2. Animals—Fiction. 3. Compassion—
Fiction.] I Title.
PZ7.B9658Ce 1991
[E]—dc20
                                          91-8536
                                          CIP
                                          AC

Hello, my friends,
Welcome to Critter County. I have a story for you about Sydney, that famous squirrel. Today he's got some big problems.
Have you ever felt really worried? Poor Sydney's awfully worried about his nephew, Sugums. Nothing seems to be going right. You'll have to read the book (or have someone read it to you) to find out what happens to Sydney.
When you finish the story, turn to the last page in the book, and I'll have something for you to do.
Love,
Christine Wyrtzen

"Good-bye,  Sugums,"  Sydney said to his

nephew. "I sure hope you're feeling much better tomorrow."

"Good-bye, Uncle  Sydney. I sure hope the bug that bit

me will move out of town. I've never felt so awful in all my life. I

don't think I'll ever feel like climbing a  tree again,"

 Sugums answered sadly.

"Don't forget to take the  medicine  Dr. Duck

gave you. And I'll be back tomorrow to drive you and your mom

to the doctor if you need to go."  Sydney waved good-bye

and blew a quick kiss to  Sugums.

 **S**ydney climbed into his Shuttlebug and started for home. As he drove along, he worried about  **Sugums.** He'd never seen the little fellow so sick. Even his tail drooped. Would  **Sugums** have to see the doctor again? Maybe he'd have to go to the  hospital. . . .

Puff, chug, CABOOP! Suddenly, steam rolled out of the hood

of  **Sydney**'s  **car**, making a great fog fall on

Critter County.

G A

"Oh, no, what is happening to my beautiful Shuttlebug?"  **Sydney** groaned as the  **car** came to a stop. "Is it dying before my eyes? Is it on its last legs—uh,  **tires**?"

With that, all four  **tires** hissed as they went flat.

Slowly,  **Sydney** pushed the Shuttlebug into the Critter County  **service station.**

Lester the Lion came out of the  **service station** to see where the fog was coming from. As it cleared, he saw his old friend  **Sydney** and the Shuttlebug. "Yo,  **Sydney**, what's cooking? Um, looks like it's your  **car**! Goodness, what happened?"

"I don't have a clue to this mystery,  **Lester**. I need your help. This  **car** is my baby, my pride and joy, my . . ."

"It looks like it's your simmering beef stew at the moment,  **Sydney**. We'll put the  **car** up on a lift and take a look at it," said  **Lester.**

"Oh, thank you, my friend. I know the Shuttlebug is in good  **paws**," said  **Sydney**. "I've got to get it fixed as soon as possible.  **Sugums** is real sick, and I'll probably have to take him to the 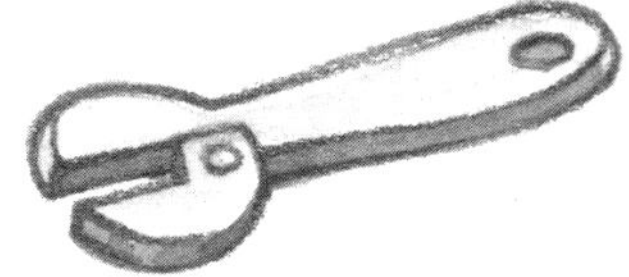 **hospital**."

"Not to worry, my good squirrel,"  Lester said. "I'm sure it's not too late to save the car."

Sydney sat down in the waiting room and picked up

a **magazine**. But as he looked at the **magazine** in

his **paws**, he kept thinking of poor, sick **Sugums**.

Was the little guy worse? Was he taking his **medicine**?

And now even **Sydney**'s **car** was sick. "Oh,

what am I going to do?" he whispered sadly.

Just then, the **door** flew open and in strolled

Liona Lou. "Well, **Sydney**, what has turned your

lower lip inside out?" she asked.

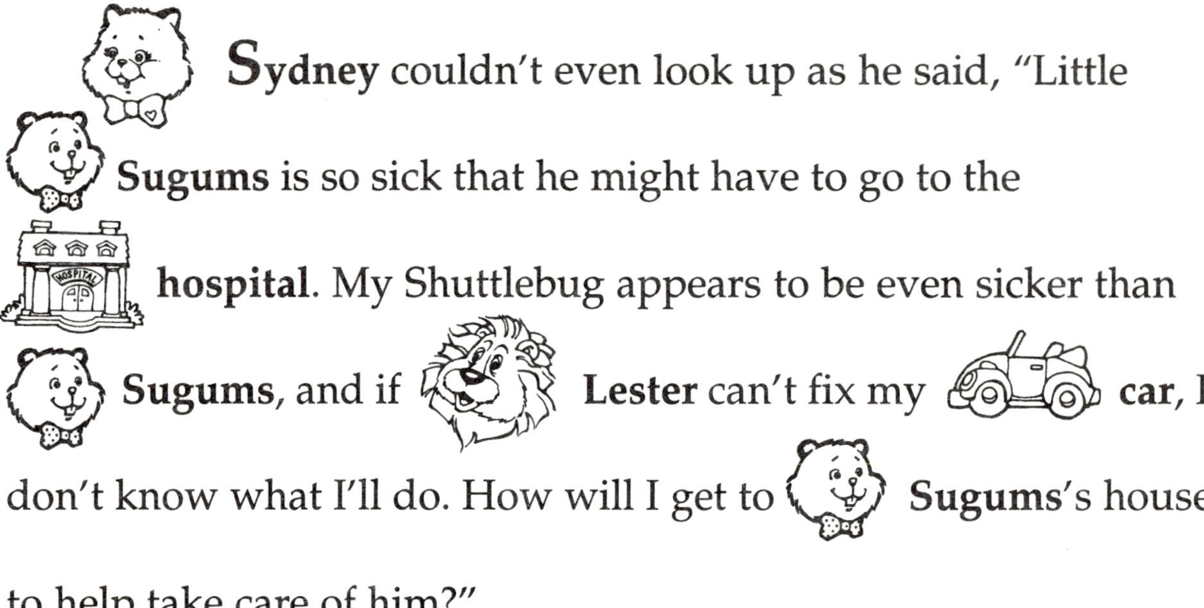

Sydney couldn't even look up as he said, "Little Sugums is so sick that he might have to go to the hospital. My Shuttlebug appears to be even sicker than Sugums, and if Lester can't fix my car, I don't know what I'll do. How will I get to Sugums's house to help take care of him?"

"**W**ell, now, **Sydney**, let's remember you can pluck an **ostrich** one **feather** at a time. Let's look at each of these problems and see how ... e solved. First of all, did **Sugums**'s mother call t... ...r?"

"Yes, she called 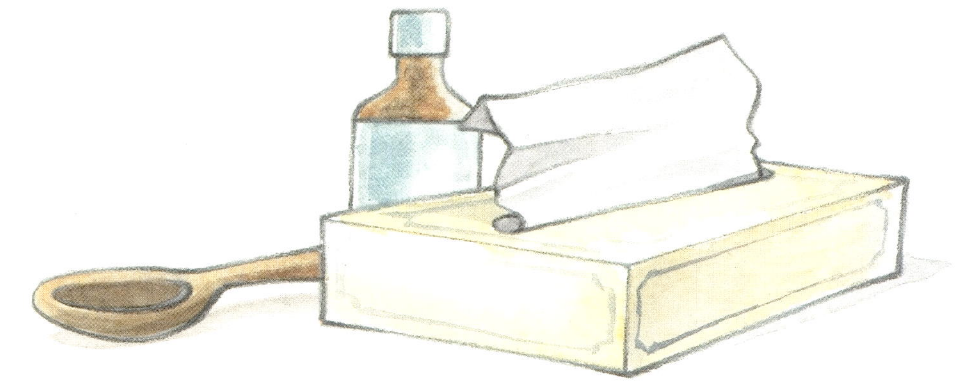 **Dr. Duck**. He prescribed some walnut-flavored **medicine**. The doctor thought that **Sugums** would be much better in a few days."

"Hey, **Sydney**, that's really encouraging. As a distinguished mother of children myself, I know kids get sick often. My little **Lunchbox** gets a fever so high he could fry an **egg** upon his little tummy. And his nose runs like a bathroom **faucet**. Frankly, it is quite disgusting."

 **Liona Lou** sat down beside  **Sydney** and went

on. "It's easy to worry yourself sick over children. I'm sure

 **Sugums** will be just fine. The  medicine

 **Dr. Duck** prescribed will probably have the little fellow

up and running around the  house, in and out on the tree

limbs, real soon."

"Do you really think so,  **Liona Lou**?" asked

 **Sydney**. "I thought  **Sugums** might be seriously ill."

"If  **Sugums** is anything like  **Lunchbox**, he'll be up and swinging real soon.  **Dr. Duck** is no quack. And  **Sugums**'s mom has had lots of practice taking care of sick little  **squirrels**."

"Well, you've lifted my spirits almost as high as my Shuttlebug over there. I can't wait to hear what Doctor  **Lester** thinks is wrong with it," said  **Sydney**.

He had hardly finished speaking when  **Lester** strolled into the room twirling his tail.

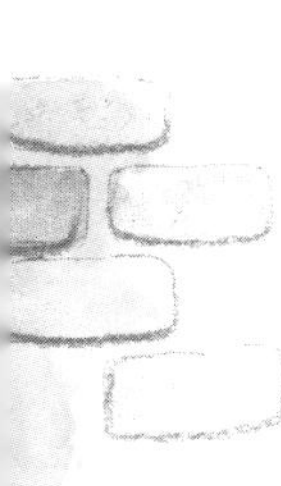

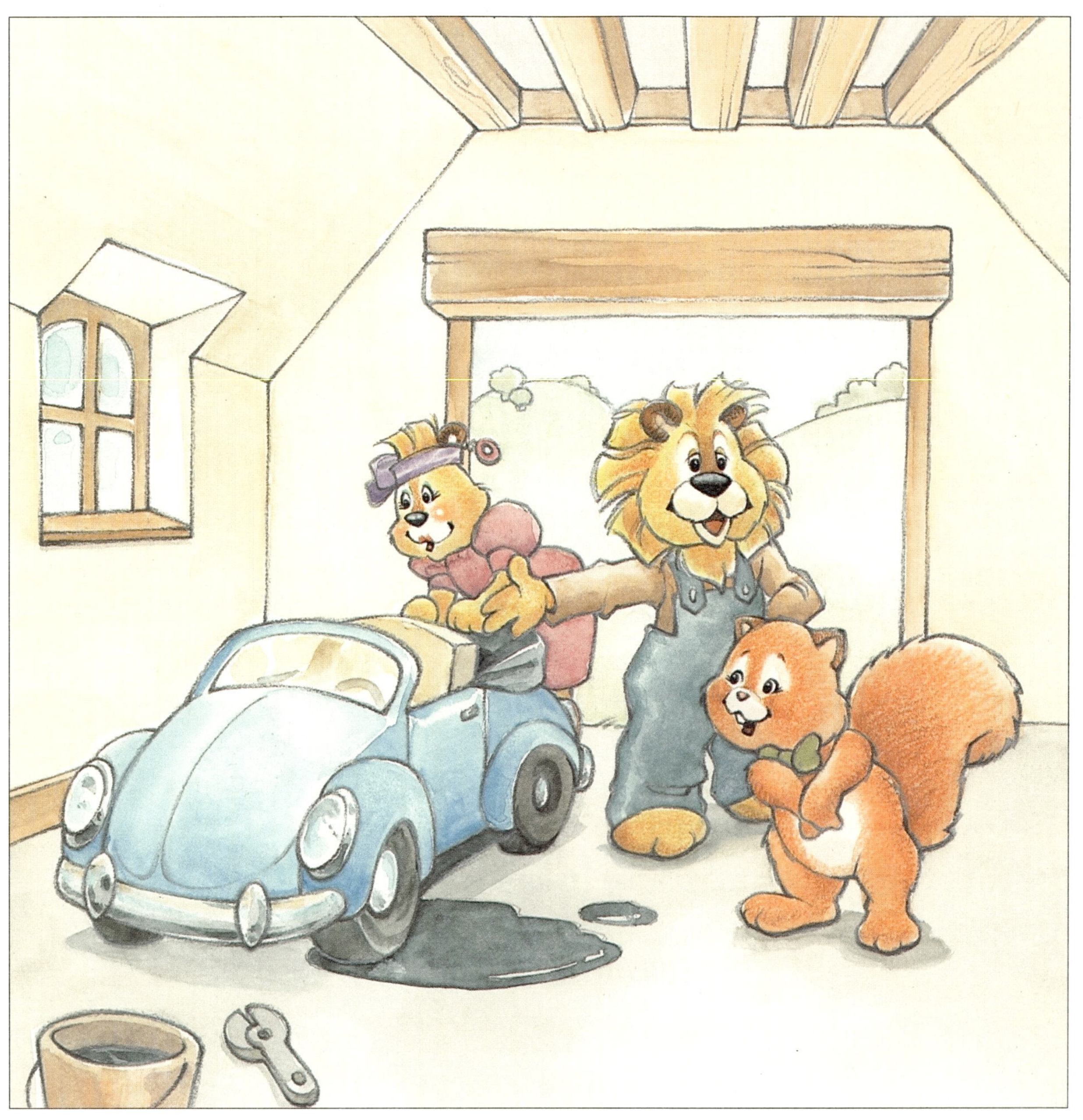

He said with a big grin, "I have good news for you. Your little pride and joy didn't have any motor problems at all. The car was just tired. The water had run out of it and the tires went flat when the air blew out. I filled everything up and she's purring like a new kitten."

"Thank you, thank you, thank you, Lester and Liona," said the smiling Sydney. "When I pushed my Shuttlebug into the service station, my spirits were lower than the  car's back bumper. The two of you have really cheered me up. You've restored my hope, and now I feel so much better. You're the best friends a squirrel could have."

"That's what friends are for, my little friend,"  **Lester** boomed, giving  **Sydney** a pat on the back.

"That's right," added  **Liona Lou**. "Now you just jump in that car and drive right back to see **Sugums**. I think he could use a good dose of cheering up from his favorite uncle."

 **S**ydney waved as he drove out of the driveway.

"You're right," he laughed.  **"Sugums** needs the same

 **medicine** you gave me!"

Hi again, kids,

Why was Sydney so worried? Who helped him? How did Lester and Liona Lou help him? Has anyone encouraged you, or cheered you up, when you were worried? Who was that person? What did he or she do for you?

God's Word says, "Worry makes a person feel as if he is carrying a heavy load. But a kind word cheers up a person" (Proverbs 12:25). Maybe you know someone who is worrying. A kind word from you could cheer that person up. Who could you cheer up this week? You could draw a pretty picture for someone to say how special he or she is to you.

Then, why don't you make a card for our friend, Sydney? He would LOVE to hear from you. It would make his little squirrel tail go flip-flop. (I think he's still just a little worried about Sugums!)

Thanks for visiting Critter County. I hope you'll enjoy our other books and tapes about Sydney and your other Critter County friends.

Love,
Christine Wyrtzen

Write to: Sydney, Critter County, Box 8, Loveland, Ohio 45140